Jac
cat

Jack
cat

Jack and the cat.

Up...

up...

up...

Jack went up.

up...

up...

Up...

The cat went up.

Jack's bed

The cat's bed

Jack and the cat
went to bed.

The rat went to bed.

Jack and the cat
and the rat
went to bed.

Jack

rat

Down...

down...

down!

Jack and the cat went
down, down, down!